Kathryn Cave writes fiction and non-fiction for children of all ages.
She was awarded the first UNESCO Prize for Services to Tolerance in
Children's Literature in 1997 for her story *Something Else*, illustrated
by Chris Riddell. Amongst her other books are *William and the Wolves,
Henry Hobbs and the Lost Planet, The Emperor's Grucklehound* and
the picture books *Friends* and *You've Got Dragons*, both illustrated
by Nick Maland. Her titles for Frances Lincoln include
Out for the Count, Just in Time and her second collaboration
with Oxfam, *One Child One Seed*.

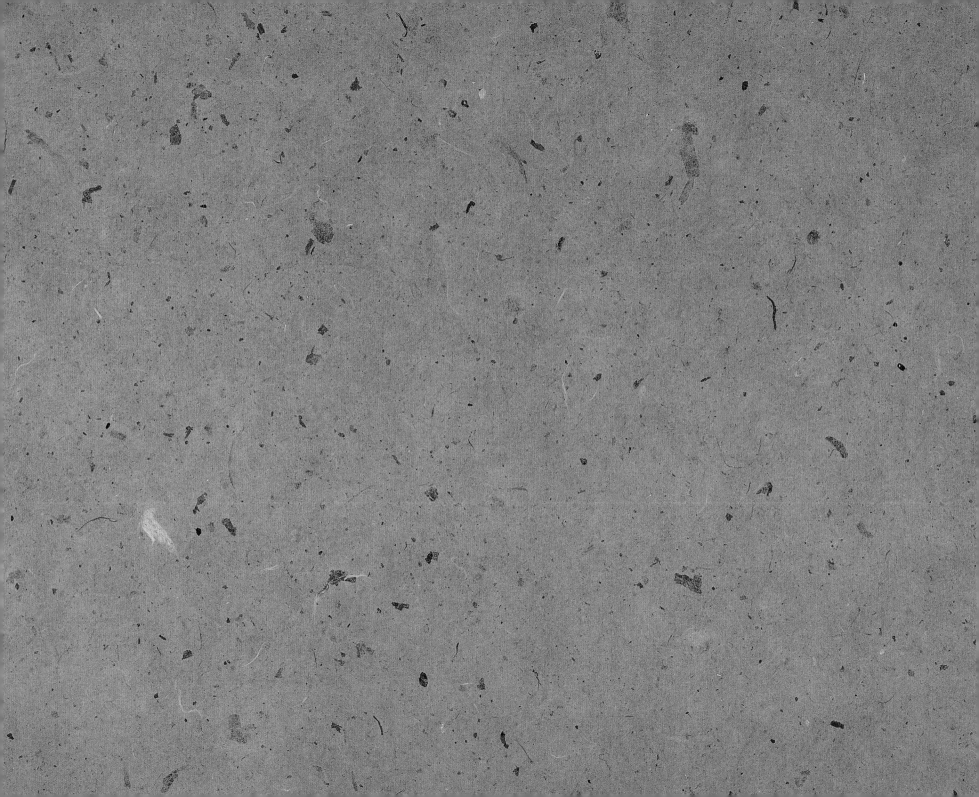

First published in Great Britain in 1998 by
Frances Lincoln Children's Books, 4 Torriano Mews,
Torriano Ave, London NW5 2RZ

www.franceslincoln.com

This paperback edition published in Great Britain and in the USA in 2007

British Library Cataloguing in Publication Data available on request

ISBN 978-1-84507-314-5

Printed in Dongguan, Guangdong, China by Kwong Fat Offset Printing
in October 2009

579864

Oxfam GB will receive a 3.5% royalty for each copy sold.
Oxfam is a Registered Charity no.202918
Oxfam GB ia a member of Oxfam International

W is for World

A ROUND-THE-WORLD ABC

Kathryn Cave

F

FRANCES LINCOLN
CHILDREN'S BOOKS

IN ASSOCIATION WITH

Oxfam

Author's note

If you look at a map of the world, you can find all sorts of things: countries and continents, oceans and rivers, ice-caps and deserts. Maps of the world show the planet we live on, the physical world we share.

The alphabet of *W is for World* is full of the kinds of things you won't find on a map. It's about homes, schools, and families, the clothes we wear, the kinds of food we eat. It's an alphabet of people, cultures, customs and beliefs. In fact, it isn't really an alphabet of one world at all, but of many worlds – too many to count – the worlds of children growing up in places as far apart as Greenland, Jamaica and Colombia, or India, Brazil and Mozambique. I hope it suggests both how different the world may look to people of different backgrounds, and in spite of that, how many important things we have in common.

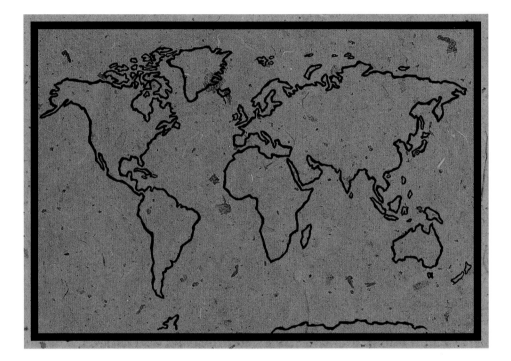

Thank you to Oxfam for their help and expertise in researching this book, to all the children whose photographs appear (sometimes under made-up names if we couldn't find the real ones), and to Floella Benjamin for giving her wonderful, enthusiastic support.

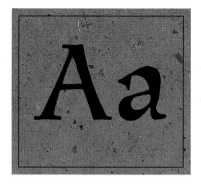

Aa is for Arturo, Alfredo, Agostino
and all of the children who work.

All over the world, there are children who work. The money they earn helps their families survive. Arturo and his friends are selling samosas – hot spicy snacks – on a street in Maputo, Mozambique.

Bb

is for Books to read,
to treasure, to share
with our friends.

Nur lives on an island in
Bangladesh. There is no
bookshop or library near
her home, so her books
are especially precious.

Cc is for Clothes to keep us cool when we're hot, and warm when we're cold, and make us stand out in a crowd.

Senegal women can buy cloth from all over the world at their local market. They make their outfits themselves, or get a friend or a seamstress to do it. No two outfits look quite the same – the aim is to make a splash and stand out in the crowd.

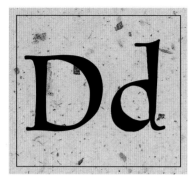

Dd

is for Desert, too dry and dusty
for most plants to grow.

Rain is scarce in the desert, and water is very precious. Without it, people, plants and animals die. The deserts of the world are spreading, as the climate changes and people use up the trees and plants that grow around them. Abdou, who lives in the north of Mali, is getting water for his donkeys from a well.

Ee

is for Eyes, which let
us see the world
and each other.

We use our eyes every moment,
from when we wake until we fall
asleep again. Without them we
couldn't recognise colours or a
friendly face. Anyone with good
eyesight, like Oscar, has
something to be thankful for.
Oscar lives in Colombia.

Ff is for the Food we grow or buy, prepare and cook in so many different ways.

Whether we eat rice boiled over an open flame in India, oranges fresh from the market stall in Bolivia, or pounded grain in Pakistan, what we eat and how we eat it is important to us. Most important of all is that nobody goes hungry.

Gg

is for Grandfather, gentle
and wise, ready to tell you
a story and give a hug.

Grandparents are special, no
matter where you live. In some
countries, grandparents live
together with their children and
grandchildren in the same family
home. No one could feel lonely
with a family this big. Sumana
and her grandfather are from a
Tamil community in Sri Lanka.

H h is for Home,
the place we belong.

Homes come in all shapes and sizes. For some people, it's a tent, like the one where Hamid and Hameda live in the desert of Sudan. It may be a wooden shack in a township in South Africa, or a hut in the forests of Brazil. The best thing about home is to have one. Home is where we feel safe and loved.

is for Icebergs,
bigger than houses,
floating past in the sea.

Some parts of the world are
covered in ice all year round.
These giant icebergs have broken
away from the ice-cap that
covers Greenland, and are
floating south past the shore.
The water is very cold here, so
although it's a hot summer day,
the boys wear boots to paddle.

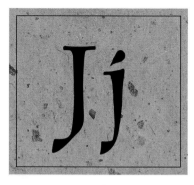

J j is for Journeys, long or short, with friends or alone.

No need to journey by plane, or car, or train or bicycle: most people still travel on foot. These children in Ecuador are setting off to the local school. It's quite a walk, but they have friends to share the journey.

Dominique has no running water at home. She's carrying it back from the well in a bucket. She lives in a dry part of Haiti, a country in the Caribbean.

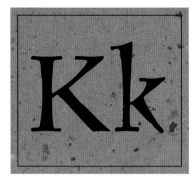

Kk is for Kite, to play with on a windy day.

Kite-flying began in China, but now it's popular everywhere. Whole families go out to fly kites together on this hillside in Ecuador.

Ll

is for the Lamps
we light at night.

Many homes have no gas or
electricity. After dark, people
use lanterns, candles or lamps.
This Indian shepherd studies
by lamplight to learn new
ways to look after his flock.

Mm is for Music, to celebrate and spread good news far and wide.

Mbourel Dia's group of musicians travels from village to village in Senegal, singing songs about the past and what's been happening locally. They make music on drums, guitars, and whatever else is handy. Who needs a telephone or a radio when you can get news this way?

is for our Name that tells
the world who we are.

Our name is one of the first
things we learn. We may be
named after a relative or a
friend of the family. We may
use the same last name as our
mother or father. Some names
have a special meaning. This
Ethiopian girl is called Muluken,
which means 'a full day'.

Oo is for Oceans, where we fish, and sail and play.

More than two-thirds of our world is covered by salt water. Oceans give us food like fish and seaweeds. Oil and other minerals lie under them. We use them to move goods by ship around the world. Where Sharijah and his friends live in Southern India, the Indian Ocean is very rough. The men fish in teams of three.

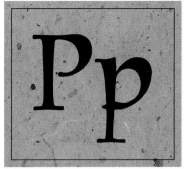 is for the Peace
we need to work,
sleep, and grow.

Peace gives people the chance to work in the fields and walk in the streets without danger. Children can sleep undisturbed, and wake up to find the world a safe place.

War in Vietnam ended more than 20 years ago. Now people can work in the rice-fields without fear of bombs or bullets. The children napping peacefully side by side are at a kindergarten in Nepal.

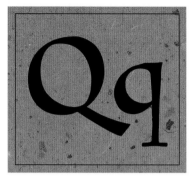

Qq is for Queue where we wait our turn and chat to our neighbours.

People queue for all sorts of things: for food, for water, for shelter, for a ride. These women are queuing for water in a village in India.

Rr

is for River, for splashing, for washing, for drawing water, for taking us from place to place.

Pedro and Paulo live in a part of Brazil where roads are few and far between. The river is the best way to travel, especially for short journeys.

Ss is for Sunrise, time to yawn, and stretch, and get moving.

In India, some people are on their way to work when the sun comes up. Early morning is the coolest time of day in a hot country. These women and children are off to pick jasmine: when the sun is high, the fields will be too hot.

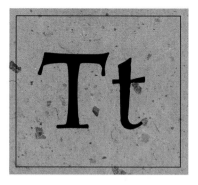

Tt is for Trees that give us shelter and shade from the sun.

Trees are vital to everyone on this planet. They shelter all kinds of birds, plants, animals, and living things too small to see. They take many years to grow, but can be cut down in a few minutes. These children in Uganda are having lessons in the shade of an acacia tree while their school is being built.

Uu is for Understanding the world and each other.

We learn about our world from our parents, our friends, and our teachers, and by noticing what goes on around us. We go on learning all our lives. Hahn and his friends have taken their first step towards understanding the world: they have learned to read. At their school in Vietnam, they write on slates that can be wiped clean and used again and again.

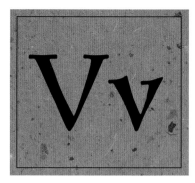

Vv

is for Visitors we welcome into our homes and lives.

People welcome visitors in all sorts of ways: by shaking hands or bowing, by kissing, or like this, with a hug. These two friends are meeting to talk about digging a well in their village in Senegal.

Ww is for the World we build and share.

Mohammed and Ahmed are making bricks out of clay mixed with manure and straw in Sudan. They will build the bricks into a kiln and use a wood fire to bake them hard. The women are at work in the fields in India. By sharing the work, people all over the world are improving life in lots of ways, making their world a better place to share.

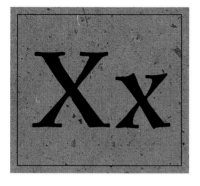

Xx is for oXen to help plough the land and carry heavy loads.

In many parts of the world, farmers can't afford machines like tractors, so they use animals instead. These Kenyan farmers are using two oxen to plough the land.

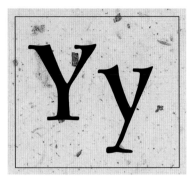

Yy

is for Yellow, as
bright as the sun.

In Ethiopia, rain is scarce, so these
women are terracing a field: building
a low wall to stop rainwater draining
away. The brilliant yellow of their
dresses and head-coverings comes
from the vegetable juice they use to
dye the cloth.

Zz is for Zoe. Like every child growing up today, she needs enough to eat, a safe place to live, and the chance to learn, and work, and live her life in peace.

Zoe lives on Jamaica, an island in the Caribbean where a third of all people are under the age of fifteen. Like people all over the world, Jamaican families help each other, working together to make life better for themselves and their children.

Oxfam believes that all people have basic rights: to earn a living, to have food, shelter, health care and education. There are ten Oxfam organisations around the world – they work with poor people in over 70 countries. Oxfam provides relief in emergencies, and gives long-term support to people who are working to make life better for themselves and their families.

Oxfam would like to acknowledge, with thanks, the following photographers:
Howard Davies: cover; Nancy Durrell-McKenna: cover background, Z, back cover; Crispin Hughes: title page; Jenny Matthews: A, H (Brazil, hut), T, Y; Shahidul Alam/*Drik Photo Library*: B; Jeremy Hartley: C, D, P (Nepal, children), V, X; Larry Boyd: E; Penny Tweedie: F (Bolivia, oranges); Sarah Errington: F (Pakistan, grain), H (Sudan, tent), W (Sudan, bricks); Rajendra Shaw/*Centre for Development Communication, Hyderabad*: F (India, rice), O, S, W (India, woman's hands); Adrian Neville: G; Paul Grendon: H (South Africa, shack); Julio Etchart: J (Ecuador, children), K; James Hawkins: J (Haiti, landscape), M; Mike Wells: L; Rhodri Jones: N; Sean Sprague: P (Vietnam, field), U; Matthew Titus: Q; Mike Goldwater: R.

MORE TITLES FROM
FRANCES LINCOLN CHILDREN'S BOOKS

B IS FOR BRAZIL

Maria de Fatima Campos

From Carnival to Guarana, from Football to Zebu,
here is a celebration of Brazil in all its cultural diversity.
Maria de Fatima Campos illustrates the contrasts between city and rainforest
and the vibrant world of Brazilian children – at home, at school,
fishing on the river and painting in the open air.

ISBN 978-0-7112-1479-8 (UK)
ISBN 978-1-84507-316-9 (US)

C IS FOR CHINA

Sungwan So

From Abacus to Lantern, from Jade to Wenzi,
this photographic alphabet introduces young readers to the rich culture
and natural beauty of China. Sungwan So's colourful variety of images
are a tribute to a traditional society whose people have faced
the challenges of revolutionary change with courage and strength.

ISBN 978-1-84507-318-3

Frances Lincoln titles are available from all good bookshops.
You can also buy books and find out more about your favourite titles,
authors and illustrators on our website: www.franceslincoln.com